Jesus gives the people food

Story by Penny Frank

Illustrated by John Hayson

THE LION
STORY BIBLE

36

TRING · BELLEVILLE · SYDNEY

The New Testament tells us how God sent his Son Jesus to show us what God is like, and how we can belong to God's kingdom.

Jesus lived in Galilee, in a country called Israel.

Because Jesus was a very special person – God's own Son – exciting things often happened to the people near him – things which showed the power of God. The people called them miracles.

This is the story of the biggest picnic ever – and how Jesus showed God's power at work.

Copyright © 1984 Lion Publishing

Published by
Lion Publishing plc
Icknield Way, Tring, Herts, England
ISBN 0 85648 761 9
Lion Publishing Corporation
10885 Textile Road, Belleville,
Michigan 48111, USA
ISBN 0 85648 761 9
Albatross Books
PO Box 320, Sutherland, NSW 2232, Australia
ISBN 0 86760 545 6

First edition 1984

Printed and bound in Hong Kong
by Mandarin Offset International (HK) Ltd.

British Library Cataloguing in Publication Data

Frank, Penny
  Jesus gives the people food. – (The
  Lion Story Bible; 36)
  1. Feeding of the five thousand
  (Miracle) – Juvenile literature
  I. Title   II. Haysom, John
  226'.709505   BT367.F4

ISBN 0-85648-761-9

Many people crowded to hear Jesus. They liked to listen to what he said about God's kingdom. And Jesus loved to talk to them.

Some of the special friends of Jesus
were fishermen on Lake Galilee. They
liked taking Jesus out fishing with them.

One day they took Jesus across the lake
in their boat, to get away from the
crowds. But when they got to the other
side, they found that the people had run
round the lake to meet them.

There was a great crowd. Some of them
were poor people who had no money or
jobs. Others were rich and wore
expensive clothes.

The children had a wonderful time.
They ran on the grass and hid behind
rocks. When they were tired they made
their way through the crowd of grown-
ups until they were close to Jesus. They
all listened to him.

'Look,' said Jesus to the grown-ups, 'to come into God's kingdom you must be like one of these little children. Then God will welcome you.'

'But what is his kingdom like?' asked the people.

'It is like a beautiful pearl,' said Jesus.
'Once you have seen it you are ready to
give all you have in order to own it.'
  'What a wonderful kingdom,'
everyone said.

By the time the evening came they were
a long way from the nearest town and
everyone was very hungry.

Jesus' friends wanted him to send the people home but Jesus said, 'No, they need some food before they go. You must give them something to eat.'

'How can we?' said his friends. 'There are so many people here.'

The friends talked together. They were
worried. There were no shops in the
hills, and anyway they had no money
to buy so much food.

A little boy who had been with them all day came up to them.

'I forgot to eat my food because I was listening to Jesus. Would you like it?'

When Jesus took the food he did not eat it himself. He told his friends to make the people sit down on the grass. They must get ready for a great big picnic.

The friends did as Jesus told them but they knew that all Jesus had was the boy's food. There were only five little rolls and two small fish.

'It's not even enough for us,' they said.

Then Jesus stood up and said thank you to God for giving them food.

Jesus picked up the boy's little basket
and said to his friends, 'You will need a
basket each to take food to all these
people.'

Jesus laughed. 'Look how far you have to carry it,' and he pointed up the hill to all the people.

Each friend had a basket. Each one took some of the rolls and fish in his basket. They obeyed Jesus.

Each friend went to a different part of the hillside. They started to give food to the people.

At first they only gave tiny pieces to everyone.

Then they found they had enough to give a second helping.

Soon they saw that there was plenty of food for all the people at the picnic.

The friends stopped looking worried.
They smiled. Then they laughed. It was
just like a party.

The little boy was very pleased he
had not had time to eat his food.

When the picnic was over everyone
helped to pick up the scraps.

They put all the food which had not
been eaten into baskets. There were
twelve baskets full!

The people couldn't believe their eyes.
'It's a miracle', they said. 'Jesus had
only five rolls and two fish. Now we are
full of food and all this is left over.'

'Give thanks to God,' said Jesus. 'But
God's kingdom has even better bread
than this. Bread which will never go
mouldy or stale. Why don't you ask for
that bread too?'

'What bread does God have which lasts for ever?' they asked.

'He has me,' smiled Jesus. 'I am the Bread of Life. I have come to give you life for ever.'

The Lion Story Bible is made up of 52 individual stories for young readers, building up an understanding of the Bible as one story–God's story–a story for all time and all people.

The New Testament section (numbers 31-52) covers the life and teaching of God's Son, Jesus. The stories are about the people he met, what he did and what he said. Almost all we know about the life of Jesus is recorded in the four Gospels–Matthew, Mark, Luke and John. The word gospel means 'good news'.

The last four stories in this section are about the first Christians, who started to tell others the 'good news', as Jesus had commanded them–a story which continues today all over the world.

Jesus gives the people food is from John's Gospel, chapter 6. This miracle is often called 'the feeding of the 5,000' and is recorded in all four Gospels.

John links the story with Jesus' words, 'Those who come to me will never be hungry. Everyone who believes has eternal life. I am the bread of life.' Jesus came, not just to feed the hungry but to give life to the world.

The next story in this series, number 37: *Secrets Jesus told,* is all about God's kingdom.